Social-Democra

Woman Suffi

A Paper Read by Clara Zetkin to the Conference of
Women Belonging to the Social-Democratic Party Held at
Mannheim, Before the Opening of the Annual Congress of
the German Social-Democracy

Klara Zetkin

Alpha Editions

This edition published in 2023

ISBN : 9789357967402

Design and Setting By
Alpha Editions
www.alphaedis.com
Email - info@alphaedis.com

Social-Democracy & Woman Suffrage.

A PAPER READ BY

CLARA ZETKIN

To the Conference of Women belonging to the Social-Democratic Party held at Mannheim, before the opening of the Annual Congress of the German Social-Democracy.

Comrades,—The decision to discuss the question of Woman Suffrage at this Congress was not arrived at from any theoretical considerations, or from any wish to point out the advisability of such a measure. This desirability has long been acknowledged by Social-Democrats, and by the women who work with them for the attainment of their aims. We have been much more interested in the tactics and in the historical events about which I am now going to speak. There never was greater urgency than at the present time for making the question of Woman Suffrage one of the chief demands of our practical programme in politics. It is well for us, therefore, to be clear that we are on the right lines, and in what conditions and in what ways we should conduct the agitation, the action, the struggle for Woman Suffrage so as to bring it before the public as a question of intense practical activity for all. But we should not be what we are, we should not be working-class women agitators who base their demands on the ground of a Socialist demand, if we did not, when seeking on the right lines, with all our strength, for this right, at the same time show why we base our claim for this reform, and how we are totally separated from those who only agitate for this from the point of view of middle-class women. We take our stand from the point of view that the demand for Woman Suffrage is in the first place a direct consequence of the capitalist method of production. It may seem perhaps to others somewhat unessential to say this so strongly, but not so to us, because the middle-class demand for women's rights up to the present time still bases its claims on the old nationalistic doctrines of the conception of rights. The middle-class women's agitation movement still demands Woman Suffrage to-day as a natural right, just as did the speculative philosophers in the eighteenth and nineteenth centuries. We, on the contrary, basing our demand on the teachings of economics and of history, advocate the suffrage for women as a social right, which is not based on any natural right, but which rests on social, transient conditions. Certainly in the camp of the Suffragettes it is also understood that the revolution which the capitalist method of production has caused in the position of women, has been of great importance in causing many to agitate for their rights. But this is not given as the most important reason, the tendency is to put this in the background, and, as an illustration of this, I would refer, for example, to the declaration of principles which the middle-class international association for the attainment of Woman Suffrage formulated at its first Congress in Berlin, in June, 1904, when the constitution of the society was drawn up. In this declaration of principles there are stated firstly, secondly, and thirdly, considerations from a purely natural-right point of view, which were inspired from a sentimentalist standpoint due to idealistic considerations, and it will need other grounds of action, other considerations, other ideals if the masses are ever to be reached. It was only when they came to the fourth clause, after talking about the economic revolution of society, that they began to think about the industrial activity of women. But in what connection? There it was stated that Woman Suffrage is required, owing to the increase of wealth, which has been attained by the labours of women. Comrades, I declare that the strongest and greatest demand for women's rights is not due to the increase of wealth among women, but that it is based on the poverty, on the need, on the misery of the great mass of women. We must reject with all our might this middle-class agitation of women, which is only a renewed idle prattling about national wealth. If you simply argue from the point of view of natural rights, then we should be justified in adapting the words which Shakespeare puts into the mouth of Shylock. We might say, "Hath not a woman eyes? Hath not a woman hands, organs, dimensions, senses, affections, passions, fed with the same food, hurt with the same weapons, subject to the same diseases, healed by the same means, warmed and cooled by the same winter and summer as a *man* is? If you prick us, do we not bleed? If you tickle us, do we not laugh? If you poison us, do we not die?" But, comrades, though these questions might be of momentary use, yet in the struggle for social rights they are like a weapon which breaks as soon as it is used in fighting.

The right to Woman Suffrage is based for us in the variation of social life which has come about through the capitalist methods of production, and more especially through the fact of women working for their living, and in the greatest degree through the enrolment of working women in the army of industry. This has given the greatest impetus to the movement. I agree that there are facts which appear to go against this movement. It is a fact that the agitation for Woman Suffrage, though in a weakened form, already existed in many countries before capitalist production had become more important than anything else, before it had reached its highest point, and had been able to attain its greatest development owing to the exploitation of women's labour. In Russia, in the village communes, women were able to take an equal share with men, in certain cases, in the government of the communes. This is an old custom, which has been duly recognised by

Russian law. But this right is due to the fact that in Russia the old customs of the rights of mothers have lasted for a longer time than in the West of Europe, and that there women enjoy this right not as persons or as individuals, but as guardians of the household, and of the common property which has lasted longer there. In many other States, as well as in many provinces, of Prussia, there is still a species of woman suffrage. In the seven eastern provinces, as well as in Westphalia and Schleswig-Holstein, the women in the country districts have votes for the local bodies. But under what conditions? Not every woman has the right of voting, but it is restricted to those who own land and pay taxes. The same rule obtains not only in the country but also in the towns, in part of the Palatinate, and in other places. In Austria, too, the women in the country districts have the right of voting for the members of the local district authorities, but only in so far as they are owners of land and inasmuch as they are taxpayers, and it is thought that they will soon be able to vote for the election of members of the local diets and of the Reichsrath. And the consequence is that, in many Crown lands of Austria there are women who are indirectly electors for the Reichsrath, because they are allowed to vote for the delegates who choose the representatives for that body. In Sweden women who fulfil the same conditions of property are also allowed to vote in the elections for local bodies. But when we carefully consider all these cases, we find that women do not vote because they are women; they do not enjoy, so to speak, a personal vote, but they only have this right because they are owners of property and taxpayers. That is not the kind of Woman Suffrage which we demand; it is not the right we desire to give a woman, as a burgess of the State, it is only a privilege of property. In reality, all these and similar schemes stand out in marked contrast to the demand for Woman Suffrage which we advocate. In England we find, too, that women may take part in elections for local bodies; but this again is only under conditions of owning a certain amount of property or paying a certain sum in taxes.

But when we demand Woman Suffrage, we can only do so on the ground, not that it should be a right attached to the possession of a certain amount of property, but that it should be inherent in the woman herself. This insistence of the personal right of woman to exercise her own influence in the affairs of the town and the State has received no small measure of support, owing to the large increase in the capitalist methods of production. You all know that already in the beginning of the capitalist development these thoughts found their first exponents among members of the middle-class democracy. There is no need for the middle-class to be ashamed of this, that they—in the time of their youth—still dreamed their dreams, and that their more advanced members were brave fighters in the struggle for women's rights. We see, moreover, people in England arguing in favour of Woman Suffrage as a personal right. We see them also striving like the

French middle-class, which achieved their political emancipation over the body of Louis Capet.

We see that they fought with great energy during the struggle in North America for the abolition of slavery. Briefly, in all those periods in which the middle-class agitated for the complete attainment of democratic principles as a means of effecting its own political emancipation and securing power, it also fought for the recognition of equal rights for women. But with whatever zeal and whatever trouble and whatever energy this question of the rights of women was demanded by the middle-class, yet it was not till the advent of Socialism that the struggle began in earnest. Already in 1792 Mary Wollstonecraft, in her celebrated work, "The Claims of Woman," already in 1787, Condorcet, in his Letters from a Citizen of Newhaven,[1] had claimed equal rights for women; and the cause also received an impetus from the French Revolution. The demand for Woman's Suffrage was inscribed among the list of reforms desired by some electors at the French Revolution, and a petition asking for it was also presented to the National Assembly. But this body contented itself by issuing a platonic declaration that it relegated the question to the consideration of mothers and daughters. But in 1793 the Committee of Public Safety, on the motion of Amar, dissolved all the women's organisations, and forbade their meetings. Then the French middle-classes gave up the struggle for Woman Suffrage; and the first Socialists—the Utopians—Saint Simon and Fourier, and their disciples, took up the cause. In 1848 Victor Considérant, in 1851 Pierre Leroux, agitated concerning this question. But they received no encouragement, and their arguments were received with scorn and derision. In the English Parliament in 1866 a numerously signed petition in favour of Woman Suffrage was first presented by John Stuart Mill, one of the most enlightened minds of the democratic middle-class.

> 1. "Letters from a Citizen of Newhaven to a Citizen of Virginia on the Uselessness of Dividing the Legislative Power in Several Bodies."

These struggles for the emancipation of women have indeed secured some concessions, and many advantages have been gained; but the political emancipation of the female sex to-day, and especially in industrial lands, is as far off as ever, while the most stalwart exponents of middle-class democracy for men, having attained most of their demands, are no longer clamouring, as during the fight, for equal rights for women. The preliminary condition for success is that there should be a great increase in capitalist production. It stands in the closest relation with the revolutionising of the household. With the increase of industry, which in primitive conditions was carried on in the family, and when that family carried out industrial operations as a whole in the home, there was not then a demand for the emancipation of woman from the family and the household, and women did not then, always living at home, feel the need for political power. The same machinery which drove with decisive power the home industries from the family, allowed woman to become an active worker outside the home, and her advent on the labour market produced not only new economic, but also new social, effects. The destruction of the old middle-class woman's world has created, of necessity, a new moral purpose in women's lives, in order to secure to them new advantages. Therefore, the middle-class woman's world was compelled to recognise the necessity of advocating the political emancipation of women as a precious and useful weapon, and with its help to endeavour to procure changes in the law, so that man should no longer enjoy a monopoly, and prevent women from earning their living. In the proletarian women's world the need, so far from being less, was indeed much greater to obtain political power, and they advocated complete political emancipation. Hundreds of thousands, nay millions, of women workers have been exploited by capitalist methods. Statistics are there to show how in all capitalist countries women are more and more going into the labour market. In Germany, the last census (that of 1895) gives the number of women working as 6,578,350, and of these the workers in factories, etc., were no less than 5,293,277. In Austria, in 1890, there were 6,245,073 women working, and of these there were 5,310,639 working in factories; in France, in 1890, the numbers were 5,191,084 and 3,584,518; in the United States, in 1890, 3,914,571 and 2,864,818; in England and Wales, in 1891, 4,016,571 and 3,113,256.

This I only give as an illustration, not only to show that women deserve the suffrage, but also to show what importance the labour of women has attained. It is evident that the question of woman's rights must be greatly influenced, owing to the fact of so many women being in the labour market. Hundreds of thousands of working women who labour with their brains are just as much exploited by the action of capitalists and middle-men as the millions of women who work with their hands, because the whole capitalist class hangs together, and defends its interests. By this economic process, women have also been taught to think and act for themselves. And they now demand Universal Suffrage as a social necessity of life as the aim and means which will give them a stimulus to obtain protection and improvement by obtaining an improvement in their economic and moral interests. But when we place the demand for Woman Suffrage in the front as a social necessity, we also argue that it should be granted to us as a self-evident act of justice. Woman is not only now emancipated from the family and the home, but she is determined to use the activity of her brain and hand in order, just as man, to improve her mental and social position, for the clear light which the furnace of great factories has thrown on the path of woman has made her conscious of the social worth of her activity, and has directed it into other channels. It has taught her the great social importance and the great social worth of her career as a mother and the educator of youth. For the multitude of women who go to factories will generally become wives; they then will become mothers and bear children, and they know that the care which they give to their new-born children, the zeal with which they discharge their duties in training children, shows that the service rendered by the mother in the home is no private service simply to her husband, but an activity which is of the highest social importance.

Because millions are condemned, not through their own fault, not through a want of their motherly instinct, but owing to the pressure of capitalist influence, to forego their bodily, spiritual, and moral good, then, as a consequence, there is a great increase in infant mortality, and children do not receive proper attention in their tender years. All this proves the high social worth of labour which woman performs in the producing and rearing of children. The demand for Woman Suffrage is only a phase of the demand that their high social worth should be more adequately recognised.

But they base this right also on the ground of the democratic principle in its widest bearing, not only on the fact that the same duties demand equal rights, but we also say that it would be criminal for the democracy not to use all the strength which women have in order that by their work of head and hand they may take part in the service of the community.

We do not maintain, like certain advocates of women's rights, that men and women should have the same rights because they are alike. No; I am of opinion that in bodily strength, in spiritual insight, and in intellectual aims, we are very different. But to be different does not necessarily imply inferiority, and if it be true that we think, act, and feel differently, then we say that this is another reason which condemns the action of men in the past, and a reason why we should try and improve society.

From this point of view of history, we demand the political equality of women and the right to vote as a recognition of the political rights due to our sex. This is a question which applies to the whole of women without exception. All women, whatever be their position, should demand political equality as a means of a freer life, and one calculated to yield rich blessings to society. Besides, in the women's world, as well as in the men's world, there exists the class law and the class struggle, and it appears as fully established that sometimes between the Socialist working women and those belonging to the middle class there may be antagonisms. For women the Suffrage has practically an entirely different meaning according to the conditions under which they live. It may indeed be said that the value of the Suffrage depends, in most cases, on the property they possess. If women happen to have a large property, the sooner they can hope to attain political rights, because they can bring more pressure to bear by the very fact of being rich. The question is also one of great importance for the women of the middle class. A large number of them are not in the same pleasant position as their richer sisters who have not to get their living by their own work. Often, however, they do not depend so much on their work for a means of living, but they engage in work rather to increase their wealth. Naturally, they think a great deal of their class and their position, and do not imagine that by any possibility they might become working women, either employed in factories or the land, because they are earning their bread in so-called free or liberal callings. The same equality of opportunity with man, and the possibility of exercising these callings will often, as far as women are concerned, be hindered by social customs if not by legal impediments. Therefore, it behoves the women of the middle classes, women living in fair comfort, to agitate for the possession of the Suffrage in order to pull down the legal fetters which in some way hinder their development or cripple their energies. This middle class should agitate for the Suffrage, not only in their own interests, in order to weaken the power of the male sex, but they should also labour in the cause of the whole of social reform, and give what help they can in that matter. But while we are ready as Socialists to use all our political might to bring about this change, yet we are bound to notice the difference between us and them. The middle-class women really wish to obtain this social reform, because they think it is a measure which will strengthen and support the whole of middle-class society. The working women demand the Suffrage, not only to defend their economic and moral interests of life, but they wish for it not only as a help against the oppression of their class by men, and they are particularly eager for it in order to aid in the struggle against the capitalist classes. And they ask for this social reform not in order to prop up the middle class society and the capitalist system. We demand equal political rights with men in order that, with them, we may together cast off the chains which bind us, and that we may thus overthrow and destroy this society. These reasons show us clearly why, up till now, the middle-class women have not been in favour of universal, equal, secret, and direct voting for all legislative bodies without distinction of sex. Besides, as soon as this simple principle of Woman Suffrage is adopted, then all the nonsense about the weakness of woman falls to the ground. The difference of social classification has been the cause that the middle class demand for women's rights has never really fallen into line with the majority of the women workers who demand the Suffrage, because the upper ten thousand have never really been anxious to obtain political equality with man. Much less is it right that the middle-class women's movement should calmly and placidly be enthroned in the clouds, far above party strife, in the clear heights of blameless rectitude and freedom from party spirit. The world congress for women's rights has yielded a fine crop of fallacies. Carefully have its members embarked on a sea of perplexities, and have declared in a spick and span manner what kind of Suffrage they wished for. The President of the Society of German Women has indeed revealed herself more radical than the women of the radical middle class, for she at all events has said that she not only wanted a vote, but that she was in favour of universal, equal, secret, and direct Suffrage for both men and women. Of the other middle-class women groups, not one has shown itself in favour of this cardinal point of the Suffrage. For while not a single one of these ladies has discussed the question of Universal Suffrage, the President of the united organisation has declared, personally, that she is only in favour of a vote which shall be the same for men and for women. This declaration certainly honours the person who made it, but it cannot alter our position with reference to the middle-class women who are in favour of obtaining the vote. It cannot be otherwise as long as these women will not fall into line and advocate the measures of which we are in favour. I remember how, in the winter of 1901, the Radical Women's Union, "The Welfare of Women," sent in a petition to the Prussian Landtag asking that the right of voting for that body might be granted to women, but only to those who had qualified by living for one year in the constituency, and who paid a certain sum, however small, in direct taxation. The meaning of that is clear, that for this, as for other bodies, the franchise should only be granted to ladies and not to the working women, who are without property. As you know, many people would be in favour of that; and not only would working women not get the vote, but the next step would be to deprive men of their vote, for that is what is behind that idea of granting votes only to people who pay taxes. Yet such a scheme is palpably absurd, for I would ask—do not the poor pay taxes? They do, and it is the ruling classes who receive them.

The Radical Women's Union, to which I have referred, have shown that they are not in favour of Woman Suffrage as we understand it, because, in 1903, when there were elections to the Reichstag, their union worked for middle-class Progressives and Liberals, and opposed the Socialist candidates. I will not here argue the question any further. The fact has, moreover, been admitted on the middle-class side, and the middle-class woman's union has been guilty of the shameful fact of supporting, in Hamburg, the middle-class candidate, though his opponent was Bebel, who has been one of the first and most strenuous fighters in the cause of the complete emancipation of woman. This is admitted, and, to add to their shame and treachery, it is also to be said that they have supported candidates of the middle-class Liberals in opposition to other Social-Democrats. I will now tell you what that means by reminding you that in the last election for the Bavarian Landtag the Association for Women's Rights supported the National Liberal candidates, though they were declared enemies and opponents of the extension of the Suffrage to women, which was advocated in Bavaria by the Social-Democrats and also by the Centre Party.

In the beginning of August, the International Congress for Women held its sittings at Copenhagen. At this Congress, not only questions of organisation and of propaganda were discussed, but also the much more important question what badge the members of the Union for Woman Suffrage should wear. But the Congress did not say a word about the question of Universal Suffrage, and failed to say clearly what they thought about the matter. This is the more remarkable because the delegates from Finland and Hungary had declared that the struggle for the political emancipation of women had made most progress in those countries where it was advocated in concert with the demand for Universal Suffrage, especially when the minds of men were influenced by that demand urged on behalf of the proletariat. Here, again, where there was an opportunity to join hands with us, and to press on our just claims, they have adopted a cowardly attitude instead of a plain, straightforward one. The middle-class advocates of women's rights, also, always say that the Social-Democrats are unwilling champions of the cause of Woman Suffrage, but that the Progressives and the National Liberals are best supporters for the political equality of women. In order to support this assertion against the Socialists, they say that abroad some of the women leaders of the Social-Democracy have been lukewarm, or at all events critical, on the question of female Suffrage, and that, owing to tactical exigencies, in some countries the struggle for women's rights has been kept somewhat in the background. But as to this opinion, as to the action of the German Social-Democracy, they are unable to bring the slightest evidence by which to support their charge. The German Social-Democratic Party brought forward, for the first time in 1895, in the Reichstag, a motion advocating universal, equal, secret, and direct Suffrage, without distinction of sex, in all the States of the German Empire. Our comrades in Saxony brought forward the same resolution in their local Parliament. I need not refer further to the action of our comrades in Bavaria and other States; but I may again call attention to the fact that while our party this year organised meetings demanding that in every State of Germany the legislative bodies should be elected by Universal Suffrage, they also insisted that women should also have the vote equally with men. This claim has been advocated in the press, and has been defended by thousands of speakers—men and women—at meetings, and was finally brought forward as a resolution in the Reichstag. On this question all the middle-class parties were united. All members of middle-class parties voted against this resolution, even those members who generally are praised by the middle-class women parties as being worthy of honour, because they are friendly to the cause. In these are included Herr von Gerlach, who declared that he voted against this Socialistic motion on the ground of "expediency." These women's unions must declare their hostility to these tactics if they are really in favour of women's rights, and not of *ladies' rights*. The only real supporters in Germany of the cause of complete social and political rights for women are the members of the Social-Democratic Party. But the middle-class women are afraid to admit this, because they think they would then have to recognise the justice of our demands.

Let me give a characteristic example of the way in which the middle-class women's unions try to hoodwink the public on the question of Woman Suffrage. In the Bavarian Landtag there was a petition for the granting of the Suffrage to women, and it was supported by three National Liberal Deputies. Yet Fraulein Anita Augsping told the Bavarian women that she was glad to say that in the Bavarian Landtag 50 per cent. of the National Liberals were in favour of female Suffrage. I can only hope that shortly there will only be one National Liberal Deputy left in the Bavarian Landtag, and then she might triumphantly assert that 100 per cent. of the National Liberals were in favour of Universal Female Suffrage.

When I have mentioned these facts here, it is certainly not with the intention of reproaching the middle-class women advocates of the Suffrage concerning their attitude. That is not my purpose. I recognise that they are fulfilling an historical purpose, and that they are engaged in a struggle from their own middle-class point of view. But this point of view shows that they are not in favour of women's rights, but of the rights of ladies; they do not fight for the political emancipation of the female sex, but for the advancement of the interests of the middle class. That is certainly within their rights; but what I complain of is the confusion which arises when they state that their agitation is for the benefit of the whole of the female sex. As a matter of fact, they only strengthen the political and the social influence of the ruling classes—that is their aim.

I have devoted so much time to this matter in order to make it perfectly clear that working women must not hope for the slightest assistance in their struggle for political emancipation from the middle-class women, and they cannot expect them to take their side in the struggle. No; we must bear in mind that in order to see this matter through, in order to obtain full social emancipation, we must rely on our own power, exercised through our own class.

Comrades, two characteristic events are happening before our eyes. The middle class no longer prizes in the same way the democratic principles which they so formerly extolled, and they do not see the consequences of those theories relating to the political emancipation of the female sex. That is shown, for instance, in the way in which those representing the middle class in Holland have introduced into the Chamber there a resolution relating to the Suffrage for women, worded in such a way that it does not confer Universal Suffrage on women, but a kind of vote which would only be given to ladies possessing a certain amount of property. But while the middle class dares less and less, owing to the growing influence of the proletariat, to carry out the logical consequences of its democratic principles, we also note, on the other hand, that the proletariat is compelled by its own class interests to become the bold supporter of the political emancipation of women, especially as woman's labour becomes daily more important and an increasing factor in capitalist countries, and that, therefore, the proletariat, in carrying out its economic struggle, must rely more and more on the disciplined, united and organised help of women. The organisation of women in trade unions is only possible, however, in a complete way, if they possess equal political rights, otherwise the help which their unions give to those of men will be illusory, owing to the political weakness underlying them. The whole proletariat must raise the cry, "Down with all political arrangements which deny to woman her full political equality." She must be entitled to all rights of a burgess in towns, so that there, too, women may take part with men in the local struggles. It is, therefore, for the practical interests themselves of the proletariat that they should be energetic supporters of the cause of women. Social-Democracy, which is the political fighting organisation of the proletariat, has, from practical considerations, understanding the need of an improvement in the conditions of the existence of the proletariat, included Woman Suffrage in its programme, and actively advocates it. But also on account of the knowledge of the tendencies of the united economic and social needs, the Social-Democracy is in favour of Woman Suffrage as a social necessity for women on the ground of their being in an entirely revolutionary age, and also as a consequence of social justice following on the putting into practice of democratic principles. But when, passing from the inscription of these aims in the programme of Social-Democracy, we wish to enter into action for the attainment of Woman Suffrage, then we must bear in mind something of importance. With the keenness of the opposition of classes, with the bitterness of the class struggle there arise historical situations in which the question of Woman Suffrage acquires a new practical bearing. The question of Woman Suffrage is becoming one of the gravest practical importance, not only for the proletariat, but also for reactionary parties. In all circumstances, when the self-conscious proletariat has fought on this plan, we see that the reactionary parties, more and more under the influence of the situation of women's rights, argue, as a last attempt at reaction, when they can no longer withstand the demand for Universal Suffrage for men, that only a weakened form of Suffrage should be extended to women. That is what happened, for instance, in 1902, in Norway. These same tendencies have also shown themselves in Belgium, and they are also partly advocated in Germany by the Centre. At last year's Catholic Congress in Strasburg, the members of the Centre Party brought forward this question of Woman Suffrage. At that meeting Father Auracher brought forward a resolution on the subject, supporting it with remarks which no Socialist could take exception to, and saying that owing to industrial changes the position of women had changed, and that some form of women's rights should be conceded. Soon after this the Centre, in the Bavarian Landtag, went much further. A petition from the middle-class union, "The Welfare of Women," was supported by 23 Deputies belonging to the Centre. Dr. Heim spoke in its favour in such a way as to do honour to his historical insight. All honour to him! But, on this point, it does not follow that the Centre to-day or to-morrow will become an enthusiastic supporter of woman's rights. The difference between theory and practice is, as you know, a very great matter. When the Belgian comrades in 1902 brought forward their motion for Universal Suffrage in communal councils and provincial diets, then the Clericals at once said that they would agitate for Woman Suffrage; and they did, only to get the Liberals to vote against the Socialist proposal. When it came to the voting, however, none of the Clericals voted for the resolution of the Belgian comrades, and one only had the courage to abstain from voting. The tactics which I have described are characteristic, because they prove that the Centre, in taking part in the agitation for Woman Suffrage, is not—when things are looked at closely— actuated by any principle except the one of securing the ascendancy of the Church, and that of the ruling classes. The Clericals, as they have often declared, are ready to assert that women should be silent in the assembly[2] as long as it suits the interests of their power; but they are now quite prepared to loosen the tongues of women there if by so doing they can strengthen the authority of the Church, and that of the capitalist class, which is the chief supporter of the Church. The reactionary classes are only now beginning to show themselves friendly to the idea of Woman Suffrage, because they think that, by the help of the women's votes they may thus diminish the power of the men's votes, and they are actuated in this matter by the following reasons. They believe that their power over the minds of a great number of women, and especially of those belonging to the proletariat, is still strong enough for them to be able to make use of the unemancipated women as against the men that are already emancipated. They reckon on this modified Woman Suffrage to act as a counterpoise against the increasing growth of free thought among men, and to counteract the steady march of Catholic working men into the camp of Social-Democracy. This is a reason why in some countries, and not only in the ranks of the middle class, but also among Social-Democrats, many persons are opposed to the movement in favour of Woman Suffrage. Thus in Holland Troelstra has stated that if the question of extending the franchise was brought forward he would vote against it, because it would undoubtedly lead to a strengthening of reaction, because the women there are still unemancipated.

2. An allusion to the opinion of St. Paul I. Timothy C. II., 12.—J.B.

So that where Clericalism rules there will be a strong movement against Woman Suffrage, because it will be thought to be a source of danger, as by means of it the Clericals would receive such an increase of support that the political class struggle of the proletariat would for a long time be in danger. It would be foolish to deny that directly Woman Suffrage was granted, a certain number of women would at once give their votes to reactionary candidates, and so strengthen the party of reaction. But that is no reason for withholding the vote from women. If it were so, the proletariat ought never to agitate for an extension of the Suffrage. For every fresh democratisation of the Suffrage allows large masses of men to take part in voting whose political education is imperfect, and who have not yet been properly trained as to how they should vote. But we ask for Universal Suffrage, not as a means for a political dodge, but as a working means of training and organising the masses properly.

If we acted otherwise we should always have to disfranchise a large number of citizens. The "Revue Socialiste" had a series of articles on this question of granting the Suffrage to women. Comrades from different countries sent contributions, and they were all agreed that the backwardness of women from a political point of view was no reason not to give them the vote, because the very possession of that right would act as a corrective to the danger. Allemane, for the French Socialists, Ferri for the Italian, Keir Hardie and MacDonald for the English, and Kautsky and Bernstein for the German, all took the same view of the question. This alleged danger of Woman Suffrage to the cause of the proletariat affords no ground for an alteration of the programme of Social-Democracy.

But now there is another point to be considered. The action of the Social-Democracy with reference to Woman Suffrage is more and more energetic and thorough, and the question that arises is whether we weaken the danger of the granting of a partial Woman Suffrage by agitating as we do for Universal Suffrage. But to that I reply that by carrying on a propaganda of enlightenment and organisation of working women we shall so improve the political knowledge and outlook of these women that it will be impossible for reaction ever to reckon on the support of women's votes. After, however, making that point clear, there are yet, in many countries, comrades who have worked hard in order to obtain Universal Suffrage for men, and who are doubtful whether it is wise at present to agitate for Woman Suffrage. That we saw in Belgium in 1902, where the Labour Party, in their struggle for equal Universal Suffrage, gave up the agitation for Woman Suffrage, on the ground that the Liberals declared they would not support the demand for a reform of the Suffrage unless the Socialists gave up the demand for Woman Suffrage. What happened then? The Labour Party in Belgium, in their campaign in and out of Parliament for the advocacy of equal Universal Suffrage, was most shamefully deserted by the Liberal Party. There has been no practical result, though the demand for Woman Suffrage was abandoned. The same kind of thing happened this year in Sweden. Under the stress of the agitation of the Socialist Party, the Government promised to bring in a Bill for the extension of the Suffrage, but they had previously declared, when asked by the leaders of the middle-class partisans of Woman Suffrage, that if they did so they would also bring in a Bill establishing a modified form of Woman Suffrage. The Social-Democratic Party then determined not to ask for Woman Suffrage, but to vote for it if that measure was advocated by another party. The measure for the reform of the Suffrage was passed by the popular Chamber, but was wrecked by the Upper House. Though the working men had reduced their demands, yet the Socialists were left in the lurch by the middle-class parties. The abandonment of the principal demand led to no practical result. Comrade Branting declared recently that the struggle would enter into a new phase, and that a reform of the Upper House would be demanded, and he finished by saying that this struggle would be one of great importance, as it would be a struggle between the power of the classes possessing property and those having none, and that the proletariat must use all its power in the struggle. But a struggle which is to be so important, and which is to have such far-reaching consequences, must be fought on the question of principles, and not carried on in any petty opportunist manner; it must be a fight for universal, equal Suffrage for both men and women. A similar situation has also occurred in Austria. Here the proletariat, after a long, weary struggle of ten years, has at last compelled the Government to grant a complete reform of the Suffrage, to bring in a measure to establish universal, equal and direct Suffrage for the elections to the Reichsrath, and to do away with the system of class voting which weakened completely the political power of the proletariat in Parliament. The reform in the Suffrage is important, but it does not meet the demands of the Social-Democracy. In this situation the Austrian comrades have determined that it is highly important to secure Universal Suffrage for men, and, as the attainment of this object appears to be endangered by the agitation in favour of Woman Suffrage, they have determined not to agitate for that reform. The Austrian Social-Democracy has thus weakened itself by using all its power against the Government, though they think that by leaving Woman Suffrage aside they will the easier obtain Manhood Suffrage. I do not know how the idea originated that by foregoing the demand for Woman Suffrage they would more easily obtain the votes for men. The greatness of the reform to be obtained is one which, indeed, will require all the force of the proletariat, but I cannot see how it would have been hindered, in any way, by also pressing forward the claims of women. We must all recognise the discipline of our female Austrian comrades, and the help which they have given when they accepted the decision of the party; but it is still, to my mind, an open question whether this decision was necessary.

No one of us is so foolish as to claim that the demand for Woman Suffrage should have been made a test question in the active programme of our Austrian comrades. That would have been a crime. But it is another question when it is said in the beginning of the struggle that the question should be entirely kept out of the fight. We, therefore, regret that both in the agitation and in Parliament these questions should have been put on one side, and we hope that afterwards they will receive the consideration they deserve. But at present no action is being taken to show the connection between an extension of the Suffrage and the granting of Woman Suffrage. The Democrat Hock has made a motion in favour of Woman Suffrage, while two reactionaries, Hrubi and Kaiser, have advocated ladies' Suffrage. Our comrade Dr. Adler then also took part in the question in a determined manner, and it is to be regretted that this was not done from the first. If retaliation was feared from our opponents it would have been easier to meet this if we had presented a united front to our opponents. In such a question as this we should always act from the point of view of principle. For the fight for the Suffrage is a struggle for the capture of political power by the proletariat. This is what the middle classes well understand, and that is why they fight against us with great vivacity, great energy, great wickedness whenever we agitate for an extension of the franchise. They fear the growing power of the proletariat, and they will never concede this reform to us from a sense of justice, but only because they are afraid of us. And this brings me again to the question, and I ask: "Do we strengthen our power, and do we take the best way of strengthening our cause by putting this demand in the background?" We must broaden the basis of our demands in order to get better terms for the masses.

I must refer to another historical point. When in the mass we agitate for Woman Suffrage we are weak in marching against the enemy because we have to reckon with those who are half-hearted and those who are hostile in our own ranks. We must put on one side all questions which would divide men and women, and we must compel all middle-class parties to take part in the question of granting Woman Suffrage.

We must always press on the question of Woman Suffrage when we are agitating about the Suffrage. We have always argued in the Suffrage agitation that it was a question of equal rights for men and women, and we must continue to do so till we succeed. We must be united. We know that we shall not attain the victory of Woman Suffrage in a short time, but we know, too, that in our struggles for this measure we shall revolutionise hundreds of thousands of minds. We carry on our war, not as a fight between the sexes, but as a battle against the political might of the possessing classes; as a fight which we carry on with all our might and main, without hatred of the other sex; a fight whose final aim and whose glory will be that in the broadest masses of the proletariat the knowledge shall arise that when the day of the historical development shall have made sufficient progress then the proletariat, in its entirety, without distinction of sex, shall be able to call out to the capitalist order of society: "You rest on us, you oppress us, and, see, now the building which you have erected is tottering to the ground."

The speaker then submitted the following resolution:—

"The demand for Woman Suffrage is the result of the changes which have occurred owing to the capitalist method of production in modern economic and social conditions, especially since the changes in labour, owing to the position and the destiny of women. Woman is in this position as a consequence of the middle-class democratic principle which regulates the destiny of all social callings, not depending on wealth and on social position. The demand for Woman Suffrage has thus, from the beginning, been connected in the minds of a few thinkers with the struggle in which the middle class has been engaged for the democratisation of political rights as a means of procuring its political emancipation and its rule as a class. This class has received great and increasing power partly through the great and growing wealth produced by woman's labour, which is continually increasing in modern industry. Woman Suffrage is the assertion of the economic emancipation of woman from home, and her economic independence from the family as an only means of subsistence.

"Active and passive Suffrage for women may be looked upon as a social question; as a practical measure it is the means of obtaining political power, of doing away with legal and social fetters, which hinder the development and the emancipation of woman. But in woman's world, as well as in that of man, there are class conflicts which render the possession of the

Suffrage of great value for woman. The value of the franchise as a means of engaging in the social war is one which depends largely on the greatness of the struggle to be engaged in and the social power to be obtained. Its chief use will be that by means of it the whole proletariat—men and women—will be able to obtain political power, and will thus be able to contribute to bringing about the downfall of the present class system, and the establishment of a Socialist state of society in which alone the full emancipation of woman will be accomplished.

"Complete emancipation of woman is advisable instead of the middle-class Woman Suffrage movement, and, therefore, it is absolutely necessary that Universal Woman Suffrage should be obtained. Working women, in order to conquer their complete right of citizenship, must rely on their own strength alone and on their own class. The proletarian needs of the struggle for emancipation, together with the historic insight and justice, compel the proletariat to energetically take up the cause of the political equality of woman. Social-Democracy, the political fighting organisation of the class-conscious proletariat, therefore, is in favour of Woman Suffrage, both as a matter of principle, and as a practical question.

"The question of Woman Suffrage, owing to the keenness of the class struggle, acquires great importance. On the side of the ruling reactionary classes the belief grows that the granting of a restricted Woman Suffrage would strengthen the political power of the capitalist class. On the side of the proletariat the necessity is seen of revolutionising the minds of women and of obtaining their help in the struggle. The struggle for Universal Woman Suffrage is the most powerful means of interesting the mass of women in the struggle of the proletariat for freedom.

"Having considered these historical facts, the Fourth Conference of Socialist women at Mannheim resolves—

"'That in the struggle which the proletariat has entered into for the obtaining of universal, equal, secret and direct voting in towns and elsewhere, all the energies of the party should be used in obtaining the same franchise for women, and that the question should constantly be pressed forward. The Conference of women declares that it recognises the duty of all women comrades to take part energetically in the political campaign for the attainment of the Suffrage, and that every effort should be made to induce working women to take an interest in this matter, so that the question may be settled as soon as possible.'"

In the discussion which ensued,

Frau Mensing, from Holland, said: Comrade Zetkin has referred to the declaration of comrade Troelstra that he for the moment would not support the extension of the Suffrage to women. This statement was a very heavy blow to our associations of women in Holland. We had hoped that the question would have been raised at our last Congress in Holland, but there was so much time spent in the discussion between Marxians and Opportunists that there was no time left to do this. We trust, however, that at the next Congress of the party its members will declare against this opinion of Troelstra, and that the agitation in favour of Universal Suffrage for Women will be renewed.

Comrade Bebel, who was received with loud and hearty cheers, said: Comrades, after the long and able speech which you have just heard from our comrade Zetkin, I should have thought that the debate would have come to a close. I quite agree that our comrade Mensing, as our guest, had an undoubted right to speak, but I cannot see for the moment why I should say anything. But the officials at this table have decided otherwise, and they wish me to say a few words to you. It was of no use for me to protest, so here I am. I see once more how I have been compelled to do what women wish.

I have once more been strengthened in the opinion that this question of Woman Suffrage can only be properly considered and decided from a radical standpoint. Social-Democracy can have no policy except one directed by principles. Freedom and equality for all must be our motto in Parliament, on the platform, and in the press, and in that spirit we must live and act. It is only in that way that we can win over the mass of the people to our side, and exercise a powerful influence which finally will help us to achieve what we desire. Certainly it often happens in Parliament that we ask ourselves the question whether we should insist fully on our principal demands, or whether we should allow some of them to go by, and the Opportunist policy is ever before us. People think that if we asked for less, we should more easily get it; but in my political career in Parliament, which now extends over nearly 40 years, I have made the discovery, which is no less true in private life, that modesty is an ornament, but one often gets on better without it. This remark is often quoted by members of the middle classes. We might make modest demands, and they would not be complied with unless we had a strong force behind to back them up. Behind our principal demands there are our principles, which are strengthened by our force. We are ready to meet our opponents. They are ready to shamelessly repel if we ask with modesty. In the last weeks and months I have often heard about the weakness of Social-Democracy. There is no falser word. I fearlessly assert that in the German Empire there is no more powerful party in existence than ours. Social-Democracy rules the whole political and social life, both at home and abroad. Without its existence we should still be far from attaining much we now have. As an example of this truth, I may speak of the progress of the woman question in the last 15 years. The Centre in the nineties opposed with all its power our demand that women should be free to attend lectures on all subjects in all universities. But before two years had passed one of the most Conservative members of the Centre, Freiherr von Hertling, declared, with great force, that he was quite in favour of women studying whatever they wished. This is a good example of the influence that may be exercised by a powerful party which really knows what it wants.

Another question is the right of forming unions and of holding meetings. In many States, even in reactionary Saxony, women and men have equal rights on this matter. In other States—and Prussia is naturally foremost in the cause of reaction—the right of women to form unions has been much crippled. Some progress in this question has also been made by the Centre. Now that party is ready to declare, not indeed that women should have freedom to form political unions, but that the millions of women who are struggling in industry for existence should have liberty to form unions and associations, and that no impediments should be placed in their way to prevent them from combining together. These victories show how we should work if we wish to be successful. The question of obtaining for women universal, equal, secret and direct Suffrage is looked upon somewhat askance by middle-class parties. We need not wonder much at this, because in many middle-class circles there is a good deal of dislike to universal, equal, secret and direct Suffrage for men, and a very influential class thinks that this Suffrage should at the first good opportunity be subverted or weakened. These people are naturally not prepared to grant the franchise to women. But, nevertheless, I venture to prophesy that in Germany we shall extend this franchise to women before it shall be taken away from men. I will venture to say that the proposal to do that cannot succeed, and I am sure it would be very imprudent to attempt it, because if it were done all men who have the vote, and who would by the proposal be injured, would raise such a protest and engage in such a struggle as Germany has never seen. And just as the Centre in 1898 declined to follow one of its members when he proposed then the law on penitentiaries, so I do not think it will care to shake up our great mass of voters by trying to curtail the franchise. But on the other hand, as discontent increases in the mass and the power of Socialism grows, it is possible, in order to weaken our voting power, that our enemies might try to get the support of women, because, undoubtedly, there are a large number of them who are not friendly to the Social-Democratic organisation. Reckoning on this—I will not consider to-night why it is so—and that women are often indifferent, and will either be influenced by Conservatives or by clergymen, the majority may think that the granting of Woman Suffrage would be a disadvantage to the Socialists. That is undoubtedly right. But it will be our own fault if, when women get the vote, they are against us. All the reasons which are urged to-day against Woman Suffrage were formerly used against granting the vote to men. I myself, 43 years ago, as a member of the Builders' Union, spoke against Universal Suffrage on the ground that working men were not properly educated. That has, in fact, been shown to be true, for now, after having Universal Suffrage in Germany for nearly 40 years, we still have nearly seven and a-half millions of votes against us. There is no doubt that the great majority of these men are working men who vote against the interests of their own class. But no one of our party has, therefore, thought it necessary to speak against Universal Suffrage, but we have gone on agitating and trying to convince people more and more that Social-Democracy is the only cure for the evils of life. Already we have three millions of voters on our side, and I hope that we may get four, five, and six millions, and become the majority. Then when the Reaction calls the women to its aid as a last chance, then we men must work not only among our sex but also among the women. Then the last anchor which holds the middle-class society will give way.

In Belgium, in Austria, in Sweden, the position of women is more backward than in our country. Those who know what power the priest still has in some Catholic countries near Germany will understand why our comrades did not think that Woman Suffrage was advisable there at present. Yet I do not think that in those countries the Reaction was prepared to give Universal Suffrage to men and to women. But, on the other hand, it would have done our cause a great deal of good if our comrades themselves had agitated for this, and thus have made the reactionaries appear unfriendly to woman. If, then, the question had really become one of practical politics, they could have said: "We were the first in favour of this Woman Suffrage." But I will not enter here into any polemic with our foreign comrades; I have only felt myself compelled at this moment to give the arguments on both sides as briefly as possible. We can discuss this matter next year at the International Congress at Stuttgart.

For myself I have no doubt in the matter, if we wish to succeed—and we must succeed—we cannot do so if we put our principal demands in the background, and declare that we only expect to get some of our demands. I hold that to be bad tactics, and that is why I am glad that on this occasion the question of Woman Suffrage was argued fairly and openly, and I beg of you to unanimously adopt the resolution which has been read. You thus will pledge the party to carry on the struggle, and, sooner or later, to be victorious.

Frau Wengels, of Berlin, moved the closure.

Frau Braun, of Berlin, wished to speak on behalf of English supporters of Woman Suffrage.

The closure was adopted.

The resolution was unanimously adopted, and it was also decided to print as a pamphlet a full report of the speeches.

This book has been considered important throughout the human history, and so that this work is never forgotten we have made efforts in its preservation by republishing this book in a modern format for present and future generations. This whole book has been reformatted, retyped and designed. These books are not made of scanned copies of their original work and hence the text is clear and readable.

ISBN 978-93-5796-740-2

Alpha Editions

GREAT BATTLES

THE BOYNE AND AUGHRIM

THE WAR OF THE TWO KINGS

JOHN KINROSS

'King James brought himself a speedy flight and the sad
tidings of his own defeat'

extract from John Evelyn's Diary, 13 August 1690